McFLY

Unauthorized

Back to
the Future

Written by Gurj Bassi

Edited by Philippa Wingate
Designed by Zoe Quayle
Production by Joanne Rooke
Picture Research by Judith Palmer

Picture Acknowledgements

Front cover, from left to right: DF/LFI; Justin Goff/cd:uk; DLAW/LFI; Justin Goff/cd:uk
Back cover: CLA/LFI
GoffINF.com: pages 22, 26/27
Justin Goff/cd:uk: pages 14/15, 21, 31, 44/45, 52/53, 57
CLA/LFI: page 64
COOP/LFI: page 50
DF/LFI: page 6
DLAW/LFI: pages 36/37
PA Photos: pages 10, 12, 29, 48/49, 55
Julian Makey/REX FEATURES: page 4
Eastern Daily Press/REX FEATURES: page 39
Ray Tang/REX FEATURES: pages 8, 60/61

First published in Great Britain in 2004 by Buster Books,
an imprint of Michael O'Mara Books Limited,
9 Lion Yard, Tremadoc Road, London SW4 7NQ

A CIP catalogue record for this book is available from the British Library.

ISBN: 1-904613-84-5

1 3 5 7 9 10 8 6 4 2

Printed and bound in Italy by L.E.G.O.

CONTENTS

JUST CAN'T GET ENOUGH

Our favourite princes of pop have been around for less than a year, yet McFly have already been successful beyond their wildest dreams.

Ever since that infectious twanging guitar intro to '5 Colours In Her Hair' echoed in the nation's ears, Harry, Dougie, Danny and Tom have been in constant demand. You just can't get enough of them!

One Hundred Per Cent Proof

McFly have most definitely proved themselves to be more than just a 'bonsai' Busted. They've embarked on sell-out tours, performed in front of thousands of McFly maniacs, graced the cover of just about every magazine, and become a household name in the process.

Thanks to their ever-growing fan base, each of McFly's singles zoomed to number one as soon as it was released. The boys also made history when their album, *Room On The 3rd Floor*, debuted at the top of the charts. This made them the youngest British band to have a number-one album – a record previously held by their idols, The Beatles.

Back To The Future

All this only goes to show that McFly have officially arrived, and they're here to stay. There's no holding them back now!

So get set, as we take a look at how the rocking quartet have taken to their new-found superstar status, and find out what exciting things lie ahead for the UK's biggest and best band.

McFly mania rocks!

FACT FILE: TOM

NAME: Tom Fletcher (guitar and vocals)

DATE OF BIRTH: 17 July 1985

PLACE OF BIRTH: Harrow, Middlesex

STAR SIGN: Cancer

EYES: Brown

SIBLINGS: A little sister called Kerry and an older brother called Matt

FURRY FRIENDS: A dog called Christmas (because it's white and fluffy)

APPEARANCE: Has a dimple on his chin, and a star tattoo on his right foot. He hates his teeth. "I always keep my mouth shut in photos." He even wants surgery to reduce the size of his nostrils!

PERSONALITY: Honest and fun

LOVES: Bart Simpson; *Star Wars*; playing the guitar; skateboarding.

HATES: "I can't sleep in the dark. I hate it. I think it must be from when I was little."

SECRET AMBITION: When he was younger Tom wanted to be an astronaut or a stripper!

FAVOURITE CHOCOLATE BAR: Twix

DID YOU KNOW?:
• Tom is guilty of weeing in swimming pools.
• He has a lucky teddy bear given to him on his eighteenth birthday.
• Tom is a bit of a cry-baby. "I'm always crying in films," he confesses. "I'm a complete wuss. I watched *Love Actually* and had a lump in my throat. I also cried at *Elf* and it's not even sad!"
• "I once shaved my hair really short, then dyed it green. I don't recommend it!"
• Tom also confesses, "The first single I ever bought was Sisqó's 'Thong Song'."

FACT FILE: HARRY

NAME: Harry Mark Christopher Judd (drums)

NICKNAME: Juddy Harold

DATE OF BIRTH: 23 December 1985

PLACE OF BIRTH: Chelmsford, Essex

STAR SIGN: Capricorn

EYES: Blue

SIBLINGS: An older brother and an older sister

FURRY FRIENDS: A gerbil called Travis, a black Labrador called Percy, a Jack Russell called Tilly, five chickens, and a cat called Molly

APPEARANCE: Believe it or not, when he was younger Harry's nickname was Titch, because he was so small! "I was always the smallest person in my class." Harry has a scar on his head from running into a window.

PERSONALITY: Lazy, sarcastic and a laugh

LOVES: The Darkness's 'I Believe In A Thing Called Love'; strawberries and cream; brie. His favourite sandwich filling is bacon with hash browns, egg yolk and Marmite. His favourite video game is *Brian Lara Test Cricket*. His favourite book is *I Am David* by Anne Holm.

HATES: Harry hates it when people drop litter.

SECRET AMBITION: Harry wishes he lived in the eighties as he loves the mullet hairdo.

FAVOURITE CHOCOLATE BAR: Drifter

DID YOU KNOW?: • Harry is a demon at table tennis. "I've won proper championships and everything."
• If he was writing his autobiography he'd call it *Harry Judd: Don't Read This!*
• Harry only washes his hair once every three or four weeks!

FACT FILE: DANNY

NAME: Danny Alan David Jones (guitar and vocals)

NICKNAME: Dumb and Dumber

DATE OF BIRTH: 12 March 1986

PLACE OF BIRTH: Bolton, Greater Manchester

STAR SIGN: Pisces

EYES: Blue

SIBLINGS: An older sister called Vicky

FURRY FRIENDS: A gerbil called Bruce and two police dogs

APPEARANCE: Lots of freckles

PERSONALITY: Chilled out and chatty

LOVES: Football; *ET*; *Family Guy*. "I like shopping at H&M," he admits. "Is that uncool?" Danny loves his remote-control car. It can go 40 mph!

HATES: Brussels sprouts

SECRET AMBITION: Danny wanted to be a policeman when he was younger.

FAVOURITE CHOCOLATE BAR: Fruit & Nut

DID YOU KNOW?: • Danny's proudest moment "was when I was doing boxing, coz I had a really good body. I was about fifteen and in a team – we were quite good. But my knuckles went black, coz I had fluid on them from fighting. It meant I couldn't play guitar so I had to give the boxing up. But I can give the lads dead arms now without even touching them!"

• Danny would love to live in Australia. "It'd be brilliant. It's always been my plan to go hitchhiking over there. I'd sleep rough and just take one change of clothes and a credit card."

• Danny does have a bad habit – he bites his nails.

FACT FILE: DOUGIE

NAME:	Dougie Poynter (bass)
DATE OF BIRTH:	30 November 1987
PLACE OF BIRTH:	Orsett, Essex
STAR SIGN:	Sagittarius
EYES:	Greeny blue
SIBLINGS:	A sister called Jazzy
FURRY FRIENDS:	Dougie has his own mini-zoo with (deep breath!) two lizards called Zuki and Buffy, two cats called Moff and CJ, two dogs called Meggy and Fraser, and Ned, a frog
APPEARANCE:	Teeny, weeny eyes. "I've got two personalities," he explains. "Dougie and Norman No-eyes. I only become Norman when I'm tired or laughing. My eyes go mega small!"
PERSONALITY	Quiet, but cheeky
LOVES:	Lucozade; Greek food; seafood; the band Blink-182. His favourite films are *Bill & Ted's Bogus Journey* and *Gremlins 2*, and he loves *Family Guy*. The Ninja Turtles are a favourite. "People have ducks on their walls – we have Turtles!"
HATES:	Fire and the dark. Cooking – the only thing Dougie can cook is a Pot Noodle.
FAVOURITE CHOCOLATE BAR:	Galaxy
DID YOU KNOW?:	• Dougie could speak fluent Greek when he was only three.

• He survived an earthquake – "That was pretty wild. I was on holiday in Greece, when the temperature changed, an eerie mist came in from the sea and the ground started shaking! It was scary, but really cool."

• Dougie is obsessed with the store, Tesco. He says, "I've got a special pair of Tesco socks which I always wear for luck."

THE STORY SO FAR

Phew! It's been a hectic year for McFly. They've had number-one singles, broken records, toured the country – and even conquered foreign territories. Take a look at everything the guys have achieved so far.

2001

• Tom narrowly misses out on a place in the final line-up of Busted: it goes to Charlie Simpson. Busted's managers take Tom on as a songwriter and he becomes pals with the Busted boys.

2002

• An advert is placed in the weekly music bible NME looking for three supremely talented lads to attend auditions, join Tom and form McFly. Tom named the band after Michael J. Fox's character in the 1980s cult movie Back To The Future.

• The second member of McFly comes along in the shape of Bolton boy Danny. A few months later, the line-up is completed with Harry and Dougie, who stood out from the crowd of hopefuls.

• The quartet move into a house in North London, together with James from Busted. They spend a year honing their skills to perfection, before they are presented to Universal Records.

2003
November

• Somewhat strangely, McFly have their first taste of the number-one spot – before they even release their own single. They join Busted on the flipside of 'Crashed The Wedding', for a fiery romp through 'Build Me Up Buttercup'.

2004
February

• At the end of February 2004, McFly embark on a sell-out arena tour with the boys from Busted. "It was a bit of a shock, to be honest, when the curtain went up on the first night," says Danny. "Just all these people stretching out before you. But it was absolutely brilliant; we loved it."

April

• McFly release their debut single, '5 Colours In Her Hair'. It blasts straight to number one and stays there for two whole weeks. They become the first act of 2004 to last longer than a single week at the top of the charts.

May

• A band in America claim they coined the name McFly first. Formed in the 1980s, before our boys were even born, they demand McFly change their name, but the boys don't budge.

June

• McFly release their second single, 'Obviously', and it zooms straight to the top of the charts.

• The guys take part in a free concert to celebrate the journey of the Olympic torch. They perform alongside Jamelia and Will Young at a star-studded concert in front of 77,000 people. They play 'She Loves You' by The Beatles.

July

• McFly's debut album, *Room On The Third Floor*, storms into the charts at number one.

• The boys celebrate the release of their album with a secret mini-gig at a venue in Camden, London, called The Monarch.

• They make it into the *Guinness Book of World Records* for becoming the youngest band to have a number-one album, a record previously held by their idols, The Beatles.

• McFly become the first ever band to perform at a film premiere. On the roof of London's Leicester Square Odeon, they play three tracks at the opening of *Spiderman 2*.

• At the Party In The Park, London, the guys nearly end up on stage naked when their dressing room is flooded.

• McFly announce their very first headlining tour and the tickets sell like hot cakes.

August

• Watch out Asia, here come McFly! The guys embark on a trip to Japan. They successfully crack the Japanese market with the release of '5 Colours In Her Hair'. It debuts in the charts at an impressive number two.

September

• McFly's third UK single, 'That Girl', is released.

• The band embark on their first tour, starting in Wolverhampton.

October

• The guys continue touring the UK on their sell-out tour.

...And The Future?

• We think world domination is just around the corner for McFly.

A DAY IN THE LIFE

After hitting the top spot, McFly have become TV's Most Wanted. Everyone wants them on their show. But what happens behind the scenes when the guys hang out?

Tom's Best Bits

There's always loads going on when the boys are recording a show at a TV studio. Here's Tom's pick of the best bits – and the bits that drive him mad.

Celebs: "We've met so many famous people and lots of fit girls. Cat Deeley's really cool, so are The Darkness and The Sugababes."
Being filmed: "The fun really begins when you enter the actual studio. I love performing in front of the cameras."
Food: "I love all the free food. There's always lots of sweets and chocolates. We're given nice food when we're on tour. I miss it!"
Hanging around: "I get bored of waiting around in the dressing room, coz you can end up being there for absolutely ages. Getting your hair and make-up done is just the worst."

Dougie Stays Cool

Dougie reveals how he likes to calm his nerves before a show.

Eat loads: "Food gives you loads of energy, which is what you need when you're performing on stage. I love eating a huge ploughman's sarnie and loads of sweets and chocolate." But Dougie knows not to overdo it. "Don't tuck into a steak, then have a double latte and an energy drink, coz you might barf everywhere," he warns. "I did that before our last show at Wembley, and Tom was the lucky one who got to clean the sink."
Keep schtum in interviews: "I leave all the talking to Tom and Harry – they're the dominant ones in the band."

Danny In The Dressing Room

There are four things Danny absolutely insists upon in the dressing room when he is on tour.

Guitar: "I always keep my guitar in the dressing room, just in case I get the urge to have a strum."
Munchies: "It doesn't matter what it is,

there has to be something to munch on. The best is when we get chocolate, fruit and crisps. Mmm!"

Comfort: "The dressing room has to be really comfy, with big sofas and preferably a nice big TV, too."

Wardrobe: "We always have such a wicked wardrobe. I love mucking around and trying stuff on."

Harry's Must-haves

Here's what Harry keeps with him at all times when the guys are travelling around on tour.

Drumsticks: "I always carry a pair of drumsticks with me wherever I go, so I can practise at any time. Sometimes the others get a bit annoyed with all my tapping."

Necklace: "A fan gave me a beaded necklace, which is lucky coz I had broken one of mine on stage at Wembley. I always wear one." Good luck, Harry!

Pen: "I always have a pen in my pocket so I can sign autographs for fans."

Mobile: "I've gotta have my phone on me, coz I'm always texting someone."

On Those Rare Days Off

What would the guys get up to on a rare day off?

Danny: "I'd lie on a beach with Joss Stone all day. Then we'd go to a nice hotel for dinner."

Tom: "I'd take the rest of the band and James from Busted to California, and hang out at the beach. We'd surf. I'd catch a shark, get stung by a jellyfish and have fun."

Harry: "I'd go to Barbados with Rachel Stevens and Keira Knightley. We'd listen to Caribbean music and drink cocktails in the late afternoon sun."

Dougie: "I'd hang out in California with New Found Glory and loads of fit American girls."

WORDSEARCH

T	B	W	O	P	Y	U	H	P	K	O	D	U	Y	R
U	F	O	N	T	H	I	R	D	F	L	O	O	R	E
L	I	J	V	H	I	J	I	E	H	F	U	R	Q	C
D	V	Z	H	A	R	R	Y	A	J	O	G	P	E	O
R	E	U	S	T	L	U	D	I	X	T	I	Y	C	R
G	C	T	P	G	Y	G	Z	S	I	P	E	F	O	D
E	O	B	V	I	O	U	S	L	Y	D	I	L	T	B
M	L	S	U	R	Y	S	A	S	V	A	B	I	A	R
T	O	M	Q	L	B	U	S	R	P	N	O	L	I	E
K	U	N	S	A	I	D	T	H	I	N	G	S	Y	A
H	R	U	T	A	E	C	F	G	L	Y	H	E	Q	K
W	S	K	A	N	B	G	L	T	O	R	T	U	E	E
Y	M	C	F	L	Y	M	C	M	A	N	I	A	K	R

Can you find the following McFly words hidden in the grid? Get looking!

Answers on page 23...

TOM
DANNY
DOUGIE
HARRY
RECORD BREAKER
OBVIOUSLY

THAT GIRL
FIVE COLOURS
UNSAID THINGS
THIRD FLOOR
MCFLY MCMANIA

STOP PRESS!

Check out what the critics have said about our favourite McFlyers.

Daily Record: "*Room On The 3rd Floor* is pop perfection. McFly are the finest example of pop rock to grace the British music scene for some considerable time."

Metro: "This is pitch-perfect pop."

Mail On Sunday: "McFly's songs are breezy, cheeky and unstoppably entertaining."

New: "A taut collection of perfectly formed pop."

Mizz: "This is the album we've all been waiting for."

Top Of The Pops: "Their spangly, surfy sixties-style songs are like an injection of pure summer sunshine."

Music Week: "With songs this strong, they look set to be around for some time – so get used to them."

Sugar: " 'Obviously' is a gorgeously summery number."

TV Hits: "Just as we'd expected, McFly's debut album is every bit as slick as their hit singles."

It's Hot: "This album's so good, if it was a lift, it'd take you to the very top floor."

Smash Hits: "This album should be the soundtrack to your summer."

I Love Pop: "This is the only album for your stereo this month."

Daily Record: " 'Obviously' is a brilliantly breezy little pop tune."

Wordsearch Answers (page 20)

T	B	W	O	P	Y	U	H	P	K	O	D	U	Y	R
U	F	O	N	T	H	I	R	D	F	L	O	O	R	E
L	I	J	V	H	I	J	I	E	H	F	U	R	Q	C
D	V	Z	H	A	R	R	Y	A	J	O	G	P	E	O
R	E	U	S	T	L	U	D	I	X	T	I	Y	C	R
G	C	T	P	G	Y	G	Z	S	I	P	E	F	O	D
E	O	B	V	I	O	U	S	L	Y	D	I	L	T	B
M	L	S	U	R	Y	S	A	S	V	A	B	I	A	R
T	O	M	Q	L	B	U	S	R	P	N	O	L	I	E
K	U	N	S	A	I	D	T	H	I	N	G	S	Y	A
H	R	U	T	A	E	C	F	G	L	Y	H	E	Q	K
W	S	K	A	N	B	G	L	T	O	R	T	U	E	E
Y	M	C	F	L	Y	M	C	M	A	N	I	A	K	R

THE ALBUM

Room On The 3rd Floor is the most important album in any McFly fan's CD collection. Here's a track-by-track low-down on thirteen awesome songs.

'5 Colours In Her Hair'

Tom: "To begin with we never thought this would be a first single. It was the first song Danny and I began writing together from scratch. We'd been listening to a Beatles song and this one just sort of fell out."

'Obviously'

Tom: "All our lyrics are made-up stories with elements of real life wound in. It's best to write like that."

'Room On The 3rd Floor'

Danny: "When me and Tom first moved to London we stayed at the Intercontinental Hotel in room 363, on the third floor. Staying at that hotel was brilliant for the first week. But when you're in a hotel room for two months, with both of you living in the same four walls, it can get a bit tedious. We got so bored that we ended up leaning against walls with glasses, listening to other people's arguments."

'That Girl'

Tom: "James from Busted and I had just finished writing two of the songs which ended up on the second Busted album. But we knew this song wasn't Busted-ish and I'd just finished listening to the Beach Boys – a friend gave me their greatest hits and I'd been playing it non-stop. It sort of defined the McFly sound really early on."

'Hypnotise'

Dougie: "This song is inspired by the fact that Danny thinks he's immune to hypnosis. We're planning to book a hypnotist for an evening, purely for the sight of watching Danny behave like a fool. Danny would be the ultimately easy person to hypnotise."

'Saturday Night'

Danny: "The line 'no one here to check if you're under age' is a reference to Dougie, who's still not old enough to order booze in a pub."

'Met This Girl'

Harry: "We were in the living room the night before this song was due to be recorded. The studio was booked for the following day, after we'd been to the Capital Radio Awards. The message had been made fairly clear, 'Finish this song or die'. So we finished it. Because Dougie and I were the last to join McFly, a lot of the songs were taking shape by the time we were in the band. And I wasn't a songwriter beforehand, so it was nice to be thrown in at the deep end here."

'She Left Me'

Tom: "I like this one and I have nothing else to add." Erm, OK, so we'll add a bit more. This track is just the sort of classic song you'd expect to hear at a 1950s teen dance – lots of cascading guitar loops and swooshy harmonized backing vocals.

'Down By The Lake'

Tom: "This is about the joys of young love, and the benefits of getting together when Daddy's not around, because the daddy in question doesn't like the new boyfriend. Nor does the boyfriend like the dad much, either."

'Unsaid Things'

Tom: "This is all about unrequited love. Her fiancé is the same guy who's in the Marines in 'Obviously'. A lot of our characters turn up at different points in the album."

'Surfer Babe'

Tom: "We wrote this on a freezing hotel balcony, and for some reason James doesn't seem to feel the cold. So we were sat out in the wind and rain, trying to write about girls in the hot Florida sun."

'Not Alone'

Danny: "This is one of the best songs I've written. I wrote it in my room at college when I was sixteen. I was bored and depressed, travelling to and from London to see Tom. I didn't know where everything was heading. At the same time, because I'm Catholic, I did feel that I wasn't alone. It sounds cheesy, but this song is a little bit of me."

'Broccoli'

Tom: "It's the coolest ever name for a song. It's about a girl you've decided you'll cook for, but you're rubbish at cooking. Hence the line, 'virgin in the kitchen'. Then, while you're cooking, she calls and blows you out. This is one of those songs we weren't sure about when we wrote it. Then we slept on it and the next day it sounded great."

THE McFLY VIDEO FILES

You've heard the songs, but have you seen all the videos yet? Read on for all the gossip on what happened behind the scenes of the McFly videos...

'5 Colours In Her Hair'

To match the summery, surfer vibes of the song, the video featured a 1970s retro theme. The lads nicked some 'Beatles cool' from the famous Abbey Road zebra crossing. They had lots of girls in groovy outfits dancing around them, as they performed on a *Top Of The Pops*-like set.

The boys agree that it was one of the best days of their lives.

Danny: "That video shoot has got to be one of the best days of my life. It was such a wicked day! We were full of adrenalin. But I don't think we realized how tiring it was until the next day when we got up two hours late for the next filming session."

Harry: "It was hard work though! There was a lot of waiting around and it was freezing."

Dougie: "We actually had a girl with five colours in her hair and loads of fit extras, too. I sat there thinking, 'I can't believe they're here for me'. But they were – even if they didn't know who we were yet."

'Obviously'

The video for the second single has a very classic look to it. The boys swapped their scruffy skater trainers, low-slung shorts and gelled hair for neat centre-partings, tank tops and proper shoes. The video featured the guys as golf caddies, following the girl of their dreams, who is wandering around a golf course with her boyfriend, who's in the Marines.

Speaking about the video, the guys say…

Harry: "'Obviously' was shot in Bagshot, Surrey, where the English rugby team train. It felt a bit special to be shooting there."

Tom: "We don't normally wear smart clothes like the ones we wore in the video, but we had to, so we didn't mind too much."

Danny: "Dougie can't even drive and he nearly crashed the golf cart!"

'That Girl'

'That Girl' is the funniest video the guys have shot so far. Tom pretends to sing out of tune and Danny whips his overalls off! The video is set in a car garage, where the guys are working as mechanics. They meet a gorgeous girl who flirts with Danny. But things go downhill when she returns with her hunky boyfriend and his flashy motor. The boys go to work on the car: Dougie rips out the engine, Harry overfills it with oil, Tom burns the guy's credit card – and Danny sings his broken heart out.

Tom gives us the low-down...

Tom: "This song is all about trying to impress this amazing girl. In the video we're all in a garage, and Danny makes the girl laugh by pulling down his trousers'. And when the girl pulls into the garage, Dougie's reading a reptile magazine. He's always checking out lizard magazines. But it wasn't all hard work. At one point during the shoot, Danny fell asleep on some tyres, which is true to life coz he falls asleep everywhere."

CROSSWORD

Across

3. Tom's star sign (6)
6. Danny knows how to throw some of these shapes on the dance floor (5-5)
7. The room in their album title was situated on this floor (5)
8. McFly's best guitar-buddies (6)
10. The name of the band Danny used to be in with his sister (3)
11. The instrument Dougie plays (4)
13. What Dougie likes to call his mum (6, 5)
14. The initials of the band Dougie would like to hang out with in California (3)

Down

1. The colour of Harry's eyes (4)
2. The month Harry was born (8)
4. Tom owns lots of _____ toys (6)
5. Danny poked one of these up his sister's nose while she was asleep (5, 8)
9. He's the oldest member of the band (3)
12. The laid-back sport the guys play in the 'Obviously' video (4)

All the answers are somewhere in this book. Check your answers on page 33.

McFLY MOUTH OFF

McFly sound like they've had one too many orange Smarties! Check out these crazy quotes from the guys.

Dougie: "I was raised by wolves. I have six sisters, two brothers, and my mum and dad were killed in a fight with a werewolf."

Danny: "Mum is wild. She's a nutter and as thick as two short planks."

Tom: "My gran's a tap dancer… Well, she thinks she is anyway."

Danny: "Try weeing in the bath – it's good for your skin."

Tom: "We only realized it was okay to wear make-up when we found out our make-up artist did Blink-182 too."

Tom: "My little sister Kerry's eleven, but I think she only loves me coz I'm friends with Busted. She gets all her mates over when I'm home."

Tom: "Harry's the best-looking McFly boy. He's the only one who can grow facial hair, which hides his ugliness."

Dougie: "I've never chatted up a celeb. Half of them are old enough to be my mum."

Tom: "I get a pain in my shoulder, which feels like I've got a crisp stuck there. Cheese and onion, I think."

Danny: "When Harry eats, he puts his finger right in his mouth to get bits out of his teeth."

Dougie: "My mum tells me off for forgetting to clean up the dog poo in the garden. But it's never too bad, because the sun dries out the turds and I chuck them over the fence into a field."

Tom: "My mum tells me off when she sees photos of me with my boxers showing, or if I'm sticking my tongue out. She'll go on to our website and look at the pictures, then call me saying, 'Tom, can't you pull a normal face? Can't you smile?'"

Dougie: "Me and Tom are geeks with a geeky sense of humour, and Tom's a peeing freak, he goes all the time."

Tom: "My nipples are sort of weird. I've got a fifth one. Hasn't everyone? Danny's got sixteen. They're like teats – seven on his back and one on his neck. They're heading north for the summer!"

Dougie: "I don't have a smelly belly button because it's grown a protective layer of hair around it to prevent that."

Danny: "I've had a few death threats, but I reckon they're from Harry. He's trying to kill me off so he can play bass."

Danny: "I have curly hair and straighten it – that's so uncool."

McFly Lingo

Ever wondered what the McFly guys are going on about sometimes? Here's a guide to McFly lingo.

Blow out

Dougie: "That's what we say when something bad happens. Like, 'Man, that's a blow out.'"

All riiiggghhht

Harry: "When good stuff happens we say 'All Riiiggghhht' in a cheesy American accent."

Rat leg

Tom: "We call Danny 'rat leg' because he looks like a rat. It's that simple."

Go Power Rangers

Danny: "This is just something we shout for luck before we go on stage."

Splash Your Cash

What crazy extravagances would the McFly lads like to splash their cash on?

Tom: "The most expensive guitar in the world."

Dougie: "A place in California with a guitar-shaped swimming pool."

Danny: "I'd love to have an underground basement studio."

Harry: "A nice house. Not too flash though – no gold loo seats for me!"

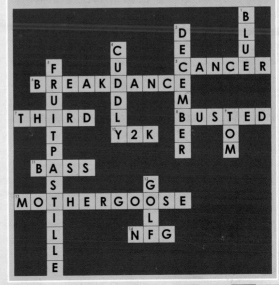

Crossword Answers (page 30)

THAT GIRL

Girls are top of the agenda with the McFly bunch. The boys talk, think and sing about girls nearly all the time! But what do they really think about the opposite sex?

Danny On Pink

"Pink's got an interesting look – very unique. Sometimes I think she looks dead fit, then the next time I see her she looks really dodgy. I like her attitude. It's like she just doesn't care what anyone says, especially her critics. I think she's amazing on stage, too. I'm not too keen on her voice and I'm undecided on looks. I'm afraid Pink doesn't do it for me."

Tom On Beyoncé

"Bit of a strange one, Beyoncé. I used to think she looked amazing in Destiny's Child, but these days I'm not so sure. I think she looked glam compared to the other two, but she just doesn't stand out anymore. Beyoncé's very determined and has achieved loads for someone so young. I'm also really impressed that she writes most of her own stuff.

I respect her a lot. I don't really fancy her, but I have to admit she's really talented. I think Beyoncé could be a very interesting mate."

Harry On Britney

"Britney's obviously very attractive. She's definitely the sexiest girl in pop. She gets a hard time from everyone, but I reckon she's probably really nice. Britney's just an ordinary girl who, because of her life in showbiz, became amazingly famous incredibly quickly. If you met her in private she'd be like any normal girl. She's the best-looking girl in pop, but not the best singer. Still, I wouldn't mind meeting her one day – that's if I could fight off the rest of the McFly guys first!"

Dougie On Christina

"I liked her best when she had blonde hair. She looked a lot hotter like that. It's between her and JLo for the best-looking pop girl. I think Christina's cooler than Britney because she writes her own lyrics and there's no doubt she's got the best voice. Also, she doesn't take any rubbish from anyone."

First Date

Just imagine your first date with one of the boys...

Dougie: "I'd probably take [a girl] to a nice pizza place, coz I'm addicted to pizza."

Tom: "I'd go to the cinema to see a horror movie, coz then she'd cling on to me."

Harry: "I'd wear something that stood out, like a black tie with pink spots on."

Dougie: "I'd probably go naked."

Danny: "I'd take her home to Bolton to watch Wanderers (his footie team)."

Pucker Up

And here's what they have to say about their first kisses...

Harry: "My first kiss was at a party when I was twelve. At the time I thought it was nice – but, looking back, it was horrible."

Tom: "My mum used to babysit this girl when I was thirteen, and I had a tree house, so we went up there and had a kiss."

Danny: "Mine was at primary school. We hid under the coats in the cloakroom."

Dougie: "I've been getting off with girls for as long as I can remember."

Heartbreakers

Danny: "There were only about three fit girls at my school, and if you managed to go out with one of them, everyone thought you were really cool. I got one, but after a couple of weeks her friend came over and said, 'She doesn't want to go out with you anymore'. I was gutted, but I was also actually scared of her – she was too fit for me. I wasn't myself around her in case she didn't like me."

Tom: "I've had my heart broken once before. I went out with a girl at school when I was sixteen, for eleven months or so. We finished the day before I was due to go on holiday. I was so gutted, my whole holiday sucked."

Harry: "I had my heart broken when I was thirteen. My girlfriend got her friend to dump me. The next day, I got my hair cut and pulled her mate at a party. My ex spent the night crying, saying, 'He didn't look that nice yesterday'. Ha!"

Dougie: "I'd fancied this girl for a year, but when I finally got up the courage to ask her out, she said no. She'd led me on though – she told all my mates that she'd say yes if I asked her out. I have to admit I cried."

THE A TO Z OF McFLY

All McFly's weird and wonderful facts are revealed below.

A is for Art: Harry's favourite subject at school was art. He got an A at AS Level.

B is for Break-dancing: Danny can break-dance and do forward flips.

C is for Cuddly Toys: "I own lots of cuddly toys," admits Tom. "And I'm not at all ashamed. I've got the coolest one – it's this bear that's dressed up as a duck. It's the funniest thing."

D is for Dean: Tom once played a character called Dean, in *EastEnders*.

E is for Ear-piercing: Dougie had his ears pierced two years ago. "It starts out like a normal piercing before the guy starts to stretch the hole bigger and bigger with a metal spike. It was quite painful for a few weeks, but I'm pleased with the results."

F is for Fruit Pastilles: Danny put one up his sister's nose while she was sleeping!

G is for Grunger: Dougie's nickname at school was 'Grunger'.

H is for 'Happy Holiday': Dougie would like the Blink-182 song 'Happy Holiday' played at his funeral.

I is for Impressions: Dougie is brilliant at imitating cartoon sound effects.

J is for Jay Jay: Danny's favourite footballer is Jay Jay Okocha.

K is for Kitchen Skills: The McFly guys lack kitchen skills. Once, Dougie made spaghetti bolognese. "It was rank," he admits. "I made my sister some burgers and set them on fire," adds Tom.

L is for Lord: Harry's grandad was a lord. "My grandad was in the House of Lords. His name was Lord Gray. We used to see him asleep on the telly during all the boring political stuff."

M is for Mum: Dougie calls his mum Mother Goose. "I call her that coz she doesn't like it," he says cheekily.

N is for Naughty: Harry used to be a naughty little lad. "I poured a carton of apple juice on the floor, then got a load of books, put them on the floor and skated around on the juice."

O is for Obsession: Harry is obsessed with wrinkly actor Clint Eastwood.

P is for Photo: "My mum's got this really embarrassing baby photo of me. In this picture I'm lying on a beach with a pair of sunglasses on my bum. She's always showing it to people when they come round," admits Dougie.

Q is for the Queen: Harry's a huge fan. "She's really cool," he gushes.

R is for Rugby Pitch: Harry used to snog girls on the school rugby pitch.

S is for Salmon: Harry once worked in a salmon factory over Christmas. "I'd come home reeking of fish, but I really needed the money."

T is for Tongue: Dougie can fold his tongue in half.

U is for Ukulele: As well as the guitar, Danny can play the drums, the ukulele, the harmonica and the accordion.

V is for Vain: According to the others, Dougie is the vainest. He spends the most time in the bathroom.

W is for Wasps: Danny is scared of wasps. Once, one flew down his T-shirt.

"I was so scared that I tore my T-shirt right off and ran along the street half-naked."

X is for X-rated: McFly get some X-rated fanmail. Harry reveals, "I once had a letter from a woman as old as my mum which said, 'Hey, Toy Boy, give me a call'!"

Y is for Y2K: Danny used to be in a band with his older sister called Y2K.

Z is for Zzzz: Tom's favourite pastime is catching some zzzz's. "We travel about in cars loads and I always fall asleep. But I always fall asleep with my earphones on and get really hurty ears." Ah, bless!

WHO IS YOUR McFLY GUY?

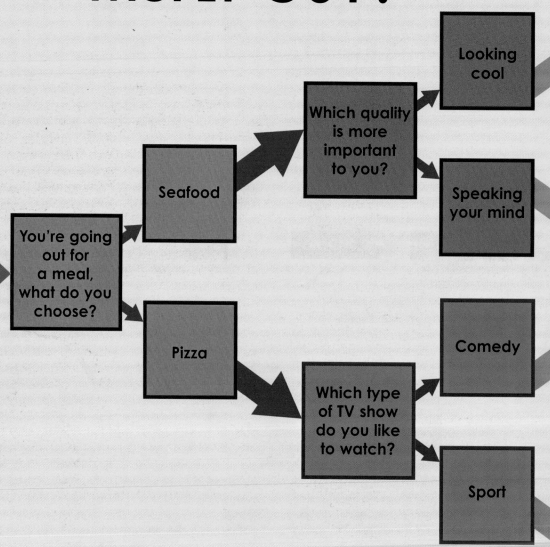

Looking cool

Which quality is more important to you?

Seafood

Speaking your mind

Start

You're going out for a meal, what do you choose?

Comedy

Pizza

Which type of TV show do you like to watch?

Sport

Answer the questions, go with the flow,
and discover which dreamy dude you're destined to date.

What's your favourite lesson at school?

Art

Music

How do you like to chill out?

Playing footie

Hanging out with your mates

Which type of music do you prefer?

Nu-skool pop-punk

Old school rock 'n' roll

Harry
Harry is your McFly boy.
Our posh Prince of Pop would shower you with gorgeous choccies and expensive flowers. He would charm the socks off you with his impeccable manners and whisk you away for an amazing romantic date.

Danny
Your perfect McFlyer is definitely Danny Boy. There's no such thing as a dull moment when he's around. This luscious lad would have you in fits of giggles with his cheeky sense of humour and off-the-wall attitude.

Dougie
You and Dougie would make the world's cutest couple. This laid-back lad would take you to all the coolest places and would make sure you had fun. He may be the baby of the band, but don't be fooled by his timid exterior – you may be surprised to discover that Dougie isn't as quiet as he seems.

Tom
Tom is the guy for you.
This supremely talented pop star would take you home, strum his guitar for you alone and leave you in awe of his pitch-perfect voice. You never know, if you're really lucky, he might even write a song all about you.

HALL OF SHAME

Those McFly fellas may seem too cool to experience embarrassing slip-ups, but they're not. Read on, if you dare, and discover the cringe-worthy capers of pop's golden boys.

Danny's Disgrace

"I got my hair cut and it was a lot shorter than I thought it would be. Everyone said, 'Have you had your hair cut?' and I was like, 'Yeah, it's rubbish, innit?' and they all agreed with me."

"I went on holiday to Florida last year. You have to be twenty-one to get into any clubs in the US, so I took some fake ID with me. I got in, but there were police there. They kept looking at me and radioing each other because I looked so young. I was pooing myself."

"I was walking into a shop once and went to pull the door handle, as you do. Unfortunately my finger got stuck in the door. As I pulled it more and more, my whole hand got stuck. I've always been clumsy in shops. I'm forever knocking rails over and sending all the clothes flying."

Dougie's Disasters

"I've always been a bit squeamish about stuff like broken bones or injections. Just talking about that stuff makes me dizzy. Once, we had to queue up for an injection and my mate was going on about how much it would hurt, I passed out in the queue."

"My best friend, Will, is a bit mad and has a habit of saying embarrassing stuff in front of my folks. One time, he was round for dinner and started talking about getting jiggy with girls, in front of my mum. I was sinking into my seat with shame, although Mum thought it was hilarious."

"I always get a bit shy around fans and freeze up in front of them. On tour, they'd always hang around outside the venue, waiting for us. Don't get me wrong, McFly fans are the best in the world – but I'd get so embarrassed that they were there for my autograph I'd go really quiet around them. They must think I'm really rude, but I'm just shy."

Harry's Horrors

"Me and my friends are always embarrassing each other by shouting out stupid things. Once we were in a shop and somebody shouted at me, 'Put it back, Harry. There's no point!'. Everybody else in the store thought I was a shoplifter, which was highly embarrassing."

"I'll never forget the time I went to a mate's house and we were messing around in the living room. I jumped on to the sofa and it toppled over backwards, just as his mum walked in. She went mad at him, but he never grassed me up. I think she knew it was me though, so I feel a bit silly when I see her."

"Every year, my cricket team has a Speech Day, where everyone comes to watch us play. On my first Speech Day I went to bat and got hit in the privates with the ball. I fell over and had to be carried off the field. I don't know what was more painful – getting hit or the fact that my ex was watching."

Tom's Truths

"I always like to stuff my face at Christmas. But one Christmas morning I ate a whole bag of peanuts and got really bad food poisoning, because they'd gone off. I spent most of Christmas Day in the bathroom." Bleugh!

"I'm useless at sport and always embarrass myself on the footie pitch. One reason is that we didn't do P.E. at school – we had dance lessons instead! Ballet was the worst, and I felt so silly doing pirouettes. But I wasn't the only one embarrassing myself – Mattie from Busted had to do it too."

"We once went on a school trip to HMS *Belfast*, an old navy ship on the Thames. When the teachers went to the café, we went exploring around the ship. We all had great fun running about but I ended up hitting my head on a porthole and falling over just as the teacher came back. Everybody saw." The shame!

THE SCHOOL OF ROCK

Want to know what McFly were like at school? Who got into trouble and who was teacher's pet? Read on...

Danny
Favourite Subject: P.E.
Education: After school, Danny attended Bury College and studied for a BTEC National Diploma in Music Practice.

Danny's School Tales
"We had this teacher at our school called Mr Graham. Everyone was throwing tennis balls behind his back that'd just miss. Then I got this massive football and threw it at him – and it hit his head! I got three detentions. It didn't help that I was laughing when I got told off."

"I used to bring a water pistol in and pretend to spit on the first years, but I'd shoot them secretly with the water pistol... It was well funny!"

"My friend set off the fire alarm at school and, even though I didn't do it myself, my gang got in major trouble. I don't know how the teachers eventually found out, but they made us all stand up in front of the whole school during assembly."

Harry
Favourite Subject: Art
Education: Harry attended Uppingham, a flash boarding school.

Harry's School Tales
"I was in the year below Charlie from Busted, at Uppingham. It's a boarding school and the house was crazy and really good fun. We had mad pillow fights every night."

"I was a cheeky brat at school, but the teachers liked me. Once, I snuck out of class to play basketball and I ran into a window that someone was opening. I had to have twenty-five stitches. I didn't get any sympathy coz I was meant to be in class."

"Someone was bullying my friend, so I punched him in the back. However, he just happened to be the biggest guy in my year, and he chased me around the changing room for ages. I was so scared."

"I once walked up to my teacher and told him he had rank breath. I don't know why I did that!"

Dougie

Favourite Subject: Dougie's favourite subject was anything where he didn't have to do a lot. Lazy boy!

Education: Dougie was studying for his GCSEs when he joined McFly. "I haven't done my GCSE sitting this year. I have some time off every day to study. It's hard to balance the two. The band is a massive distraction. My teachers are cool."

Dougie's School Tales

"I was rubbish at school. I was always copying other people's homework."

Dougie once got in trouble with his teachers for sticking a batch of stickers all over the school. "The teachers weren't happy," he admits. We bet they weren't!

Tom

Favourite Subjects: Art, music and science

Education: Tom attended Sylvia Young's Performing Arts School. Matt from Busted also went there. "At lunchtime, Matt used to go out and get a massive portion of chips and then wash the whole lot down with a pint of milk."

Tom's School Tales

"I was rubbish at sports. I was OK at swimming. Once, at a school swimming contest, I was showing off a bit and dived into the pool, before swimming off really fast past the judges. But I didn't realize that my trunks had fallen down and everybody could see my bum – including my teachers. It's a relief that I wasn't doing the backstroke at the time."

"I wasn't too popular with the teachers because of my mad haircuts. I was famous for them. I once did a TV ad for Curry's with stupid curtain hair and they show it every Christmas."

"I was a loser in school and always got turned down by girls. I never really got a chance, as all the girls liked the older guys. It doesn't bother me if I get turned down now, though – I'm OK with chatting to girls. I think I'm quite funny."

MAKE HIM YOURS

How can you bag yourself a McFlyer? On these pages, the boys reveal what they like best in a girlfriend, and there are some tantalizing tips on how to be the perfect girl for your McFly guy.

Danny

Act Your Age: Danny says, "Older girls are well out of my league. I'm scared of girls who are over twenty-four, coz they're all mature. I always think they'll look at me and laugh." So make sure you don't try to look older than you are. There's nothing wrong with acting mature, but make sure you look your age and avoid too much make-up.

Mum's The Word: According to Danny, "An actual girlfriend would earn big points if she got on with my mum. If your mum likes your girlfriend, you might as well get married." Bingo! Pay his mum a few compliments, bake her a cake and you'll be Mrs Jones before you know it.

Don't Argue: If you're the fiery type, then you may have to bite your tongue and keep schtum, because Danny hates arguments. They're a big turn-off.

Tom

Take Charge: "I'm quite indecisive," admits Tom. "So, if a girl is indecisive

too, it's a disaster. I'd rather people made decisions for me." This means you may have to take charge with Tom. If he can't make up his mind about where you should eat, make the choice yourself – he really won't mind.

Flirting: Tom says, "I like it when girls are eager. It's flattering." This is your chance to show Tom you like him, but don't be too scary and full-on. Be a bit cheeky and draw him in gradually.

Kiss Kiss: It may sound odd but Tom likes to be kissed… on his left nostril. It's true. "It's a fetish. I can't flare my nostrils, I think I was born without those muscles. Oh, and I like to be kissed on my dimple, too. Fans often ask to touch it." So, now you know exactly where to aim your lips.

Harry

Be Active: Harry's a sports fanatic and he loves girls who are just as enthusiastic as him. So, if you are genuinely into sports, you're in with a chance of really impressing Harry.

Be Girlie: "I'm quite into girlie girls," says Harry. So even though he likes sporty chicks, make sure you can change your style at the drop of a hat, and go from sweaty gym kit to cute colours without complaint.

Pucker Up: If you really want to make Harry weak at the knees, kiss him on the ears – he says it makes him shiver!

Dougie

Experience: Poor Dougie has only ever had one girlfriend. "I've never really been anyone's boyfriend, but I reckon I'd be good. And I don't mind being romantic and buying a girl flowers and stuff. So I think I could whisk her off her feet." So let him treat you like a princess – it will make him feel better.

Be Quick: Be fast with your thumbs because Dougie hates girls who don't text him back quickly enough. "It annoys me. I don't need an immediate response, but I don't like it if they leave it for ages."

Relax: "I'm terrible around girls," admits Dougie. "I totally clam up and don't even know what to say. And I feel like I'm just watching what's happening and I can't control it." It's important that Dougie feels relaxed around you. So be casual, and treat him like a mate – it'll help him chill out.

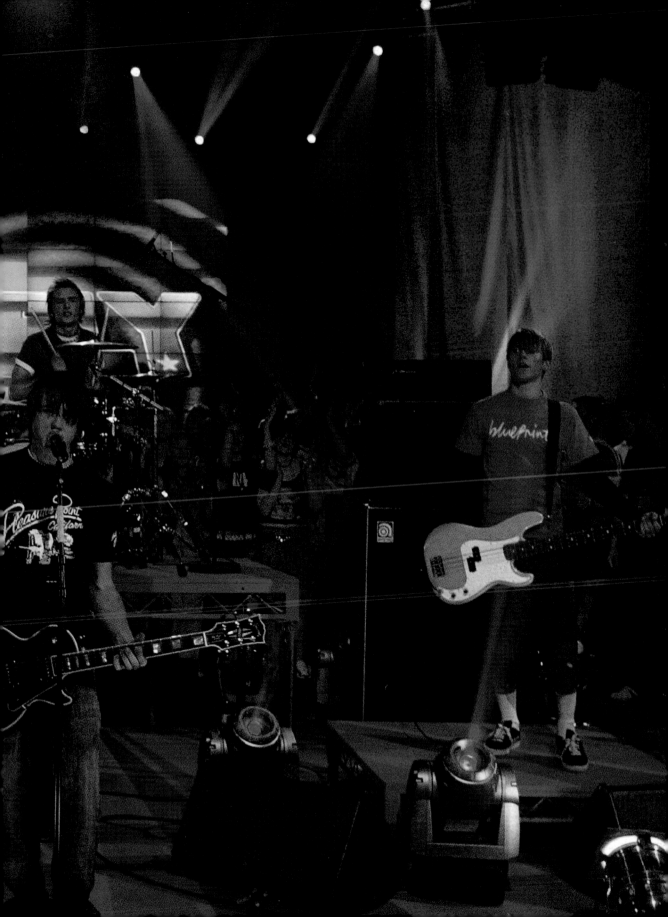

THE LIVE EXPERIENCE

What happens when McFly are on stage, how do they feel? And what happens when they come off stage?

Danny

"Even if nerves are getting to you, it's important to look like you're having a good time. If the audience look like they're enjoying themselves, you will too."

"On tour we always play Spin The Bottle. Last time, we had three girls with us and I think I got about two or three snogs."

"When I'm on stage... I feel like Bruce Springsteen. I enjoy myself and have a laugh. I've learnt that if you go out there and enjoy yourself, the crowd will feed off that. If you're having a good time, they will be too. So, I just focus on having fun. It's the energy!"

"My fingers worked so hard on tour on the guitar that one of them turned black."

"Whenever we perform, I give Dougie a wedgie for good luck."

Tom

"I feel more comfortable on stage than in shoots, as that's what I do best."

"On tour with Busted, Mattie and I were throwing fruit to the fans waiting outside the dressing-room window. We were trying to be nice, but we got in trouble."

"I'm always singing the wrong words on stage. One night, we had cameras filming us, and it surprised me so much I forgot my words. It was during '5 Colours In Her Hair' as well, and in front of about 10,000 people!"

"Dougie came off stage one night and was really dizzy. He had purple blotches on his face. I thought he was going to pass out and ten paramedics rushed over to him. It was really dramatic."

Harry

"The Busted tour was really good fun. It was our first tour, so we had to be focused, as this was our chance to make a big impression on the Busted fans."

"On tour, we like to run around hotel corridors doing 'missions'. One night, Dougie and I were running around with a fire extinguisher. We nearly got caught, as some hotel dude was mooching around the place. After that we put the fire extinguisher back and realized we'd been pretty silly."

Dougie

"When we're performing, Harry always has to go on stage first. If he doesn't, we get worried we won't play well."

"Sometimes we have to mime, and at first it was weird and we were rubbish at it. It makes you want to stay still and not move around. We don't rehearse. Our tour does that for us. We weren't live on tour, but our vocals were. We know we can play live. It's so much better doing it all live – it's a better feel. When we did *Top Of The Pops* live, we had to do a whole day of sound checking."

"When we're on stage I get lost in it – it's like a dream. It's weird playing big places and then going home for tea."

McTRIVIA

Do you know the guys as well as you think you do? All the info is somewhere in this book, so read to the end first. You'll find the answers on page 59.

1. What's the name of Danny's favourite football player?

2. Which member of McFly once wanted to be a male stripper?

3. Whose favourite sandwich filling is bacon with hash browns, egg yolk and Marmite?

4. What was the first single Tom bought?

5. Who has a sister called Jazzy?

6. What is Harry's favourite video game?

7. Which magazine is famous for featuring the original advert for the McFly auditions?

8. Which member of McFly was born in Orsett, Essex?

9. Who has lots of bald teddies in his bedroom?

10. Which member of McFly has a crush on Joss Stone?

11. What colour is the blind in Tom's bedroom?

12. Whose favourite pudding is strawberries and cream?

13. Which wrinkly actor is Harry obsessed with?

14. Which Beatles track did McFly play at the Olympic Torch concert?

15. What's the name of the small London venue McFly played a gig in when their album went to number one?

16. Name McFly's third single.

17. Who has a huge poster of Britney Spears in his bedroom?

18. What's Tom's favourite chocolate?

19. Which insect is Danny scared of?

20. What colour did Tom once dye his hair?

THE McMAD HOUSE

McFly's North London home is the epitome of a bachelor pad – a tip with empty pizza boxes and smelly socks scattered everywhere. Let's look inside their boudoirs and find out what happens when you leave four boys home alone.

Harry

Harry is Sporty McFly. He reveals, "I'm mental about cricket." On his wall he has a framed scoresheet showing his highest ever score.

One of his favourite items in his room is a guitar-shaped clock. "It rocks!" And we think he means that quite literally.

If you're ever lucky enough to see Harry's bedroom, don't be scared by his bald teddies. "Loads of my teddies have got no hair on their heads because I used to cut it, thinking it would grow back," he explains.

Danny

Danny spends nearly all his time cooped up in his room, but it's easy to see why. His bedroom is jam-packed with a home studio, drum kit and lots of swanky-looking guitars, and tons of posters of his idol Bruce Springsteen.

Being from Bolton, Danny doesn't get to see his family as often as the other McFlyers do, so he has lots of family photos to remind him of his loved ones. A few of the really special photos are of him with his best mate, Alex, and his sister Vicky. "My best mate is absolutely hilarious, we're always laughing at him."

Danny still keeps a framed copy of the McFly audition advert that he replied to. "That tiny advert changed my life. It was in *NME*. I called the number and eighteen months later here I am."

Tom

Tom is the 'dad' of the house. He has adopted Danny's and Harry's gerbils. "The boys got bored of them after a week and now they're at my parents' house. They weed on my bed, but I still miss them."

Propped up on a stand is a very special acoustic guitar. "James from

Busted and I got bored on holiday in Florida, so we bought new guitars and wrote songs the whole time."

Tom takes extra care of his Sylvia Young T-shirt, which all his mates signed the day he left school.

Tom doesn't have a bedroom door, so he bought a tacky bright orange blind to put up. "I didn't have a hammer," explains Tom. "So me and Dougie decided to use a rolling pin instead. Dougie went to hammer a nail in, but totally missed and made a big hole in the ceiling." Oops!

Dougie

Dougie's room is the tidiest, but only because he spends a lot of time at his parents' home in Essex.

He always keeps his guitar in his room. "It was my first acoustic, and I learnt to play it five years ago. I love it. I'd never take it on tour in case I lost it."

Dougie has a lizard poster on his wall, because he used to breed them. He stopped when he joined the band, because he didn't have time. He's also got a poster of Britney Spears.

Wild And Wacky Antics

Here are some of the things the guys get up to in their crib:

Tom: "I spend hours in the shower singing. I always use Danny's or Dougie's bathroom. When it gets steamy, I leave bum prints on their mirror."

Dougie: "There's a secret world that exists behind Danny's wardrobe... We go there to feed the beasts who live in it – they're half-men, half-goats."

Danny: "We've got this archway in our living room where we cut out and stick up pictures of all these fit women."

Answers To McTrivia (Page 56)

1. Jay Jay Okocha
2. Tom
3. Harry
4. 'Thong Song' by Sisqó
5. Dougie
6. *Brian Lara Test Cricket*
7. *NME*
8. Dougie
9. Harry
10. Danny
11. Orange
12. Harry
13. Clint Eastwood
14. 'She Loves You'
15. The Monarch
16. 'That Girl'
17. Dougie
18. Twix
19. Wasps
20. Green

KEEPING IT REAL

How is life treating the lads, now that they've officially hit the big time? Has fame and fortune changed McFly? The lads tell all.

How Does Fame Feel?

Dougie may seem the shy and quiet type, but beneath that unassuming exterior lies a fierce perfectionist. "I'm never proud of myself," he confesses. "There's loads of stuff we've achieved which I can't believe we've done, but I think I'm too self-critical. I'm always looking back at things and thinking how I could've done them better." It's this kind of determination that makes McFly number one time and time again.

Harry points out another thing that makes McFly stand out. "We play our own instruments. One thing that separates us from a lot of other pop bands is that we can just walk into a room, pick up some instruments and bang out one of our songs." Harry's modest about their status in the fame game, however.

"We don't see ourselves as famous. If anyone asks us about fame, we just say we're not famous so we don't know," he shrugs. "It's a bit weird. Compared to proper famous people we're not anything yet. We have a long way to go. I don't get recognized much anyway. And it's great coz it means I can lead a normal life. Having said that, if we all go out together we get spotted everywhere. That's fine, though sometimes it leads to people taking the mick, which is quite hard at first, but you get used to it. It's most people's dream to be in our position, so we can't complain."

And what's the coolest thing about being in the band for Harry? "We get to eat loads of pizza," he laughs.

For Tom, one of the highlights of being in the band is record-signings, where the guys get the chance to come face to face with their notoriously dedicated fans. "The response we get is amazing," Tom smiles.

It All Happened So Fast

Going to number one with the debut single is still something that Danny finds hard to come to terms with. "That was unreal," he remembers. "I didn't think that it actually happened. We weren't expecting it at all."

Since then, it's been non-stop for the band. "It's scary watching us getting bigger and bigger, but it's cool," says Danny. "I've noticed that I'm getting a lot more attention now, since McFly took off, but I'd never throw my fame around in clubs and stuff. I'd avoid those poncy places where I'd have to wear shoes and stuff." But surely he likes to take advantage of his celebrity sometimes? "Well, I do like the posher places – just coz you don't get so much hassle as you do in regular clubs. The VIP areas are good – I'm not stuck up, but you want time with your mates away from the hassle."

Don't Ever Change, Boys

So, how does being in such a successful band at such a tender age affect the boys. Dougie, Tom, Danny and Harry are going through a lot of changes. Has fame started to change or shape them in any way?

"Well, we've changed a bit," admits Tom. "Dougie's changed the most – he's not as shy."

Harry agrees, "Yeah, but I don't think fame's changed us in a bad way. We've all just grown up."

Dougie doesn't seem to agree. "You've not changed, Harry – you were horrible before and you're horrible now. Ha!"

What Next?

With so many accolades already tucked beneath their studded belts, it's hard to imagine how the guys will follow up such a successful year in 2005. It's a challenge that Danny is more than aware of. "I'm anxious as to what's happening next," he says. But Tom seems to have his sights set very clearly on his future plans for the band. "We want McFly to be the biggest band in the world," he states boldly.

Well, it's only a matter of time, boys, and we will be behind you all the way.